Dog Breeding Guide

The Complete Guide To Dog Breeding Exposed

By: Janet Evans

TABLE OF CONTENTS

PUBLISHERS NOTES

DEDICATION

This book is dedicated to dog lovers.

CHAPTER 1- BREEDING

Becoming a dog breeder is never something that you should do lightly, and never something that you should decide upon without many hours of consideration and planning. If you are going to be breeding dogs, then there are some things that you should think carefully about.

Breeding dogs is something that requires a lot of hard work, and something that requires a lifetime commitment on your part. Therefore, if you are going to be breeding dogs, there should be some major aspects of your life that revolve around dogs.

First of all, a love for dogs is a great start, but it should not be the only reason that you think you would be a good dog breeder. A love for dogs is very important, because you are going to be spending many hours of each of your days raising puppies, working with your dogs, and making sure that they are healthy. Loving them is important, yes, but loving them is not the only thing that is important, because just love alone can only get you so far.

Besides loving your dogs, you are going to need to be a dog person. This is different from loving dogs. Loving dogs might mean that you enjoy having them, that you keep them around and take them out when needed, and might even let them sleep on the bed once in a while. Being a dog person is much different.

Being a dog person means that you find dog hair in your soup and don't mind, and that your dogs usually live more comfortably than you do. If you are a dog person you would never dream of allowing your dogs to be out in the cold weather, and you wouldn't ever expect them to live in conditions that you wouldn't live in yourself.

If you are a dog person you read everything that there is to read about your particular dog breed, and you study all of it to find out the things that you should be doing. A dog person might joke that their life revolves around their dogs, and they are probably right.

Therefore, in order to be a good breeder, you have to be these things. You have to be willing to work with your dog breeds and to make sure that you are doing all that you can to provide dogs with good homes. You must be diligent, and ready to work for the common good of the breed.

And, the bottom line when it comes to dog breeding is that you must not be in it at all for the money. The money should never be a motivation for dog breeding, and so if this is your main motivation, it is time for you to step back and look for another hobby.

Breeders who breed for the money are never going to be good breeders. In fact, most breeders, who are doing it correctly, don't make much money at all, because breeders end up spending the money that they do make on puppies on things for their dogs, shots, and on the breeding process. Therefore, you should always be aware that the money isn't going to be a major factor in whether or not your dog breeding is successful.

There are some questions that you should ask yourself if you plan on breeding. Answering these questions is a great way to make sure that you are ready for breeding dogs.

Why am I doing this?

Am I trying to make money?

Am I ready to allow dogs to be a major part of my life?

Will I let them sleep in my bed with me?

Do I have a great breeding plan in place?

Do I have help and support – either from people near me, or from a source like a breeding group?

Do I know how to find out answers to my questions?

Is there someone else who can take over my breeding program if something should happen to me?

Am I ready to deal with pregnant dogs?

Am I ready to raise puppies by hand?

Can I be responsible for finding homes for each of the puppies I produce?

Not only that, but can I be responsible for making sure that the puppies I produce don't have puppies themselves?

Am I ready to actually birth puppies?

Can I handle dealing with sick puppies, or puppies that don't make it?

Am I ready for heartache when it comes time to give puppies away, or to deal with puppies that just didn't survive?

Will I know how to read my female dog and know when she's had enough?

Will I be able to quit if it just isn't working for me?

Am I ready for the joy that comes along with dog breeding, as well as the hard times?

The answers to these questions will help you decide if you are ready to become a dog breeder. It is important that you make sure you know the answers before you begin.

CHAPTER 2- FINDING THE RIGHT DOG BREED

There are several things that you should do when you are looking at finding the right dog breed. It is very important that you find the right breed, because this is going to be the best way for you to be successful at dog breeding.

First of all, when you are looking for the right dog breed, you want to be sure that you find out as much information about the breeds that you are considering as possible. This information will help you make a good decision when it comes to the type of dogs that you want to breed.

The first thing to think about is whether or not you would like to breed purebred dogs. This is something to think carefully about. Some dogs, like golden retrievers and labs, can be bred with dogs that aren't pedigreed. You might want to do this because you like the type of dog that you have and because you feel that others might like those dogs as well. In this case, you'd be looking for two dogs that you want to breed, but you wouldn't be as concerned about the pedigrees as you would if you were looking for purebred dogs.

Breeding dogs that aren't purebreds can be very had to do, however, because you don't have the right information about the dogs and about what they might be like. Therefore, deciding to breed purebred dogs can actually be better because you will be able to look at their lineages, and make sure that you are breeding a pair that is going to produce good puppies.

You also want to think about the sizes of the dogs that you want to be breeding. You should be looking at a size that is compatible for you. Remember that the best breeders keep their dogs in the house with them – breeding dogs should not be kept outside and should not be kept in kennels or runs. So, you want to decide on a breed that is going to be best for your home life. For instance, if you have a small home, breeding small dogs is probably better. If you have a large home with lots of room for bigger dogs, you can consider breeding bigger dogs.

Once you've decided on a breed of dogs, go ahead and do some research so that you can discover all of the fine points about the dog that you have chosen. You want to look at what breeders are currently breeding for with particular type of dog, and you want to see what types of things breeders are attempting to breed out.

Also, you'll want to think about things like temperament and about making sure that the dogs you are breeding have the right temperament. Look to see if the breed is good with children and other animals.

And listen in on some of the online discussions about breeding your particular type of dog. You want to make sure that you are getting into a breeding program that fits your needs – and one where the people are going to be ready and willing to help you a long a little bit. This is very important because it will give you a chance to make sure that you are doing the right thing.

CHAPTER 3- CREATE AN ACTION PLAN

As you begin to breed, you are going to need to have a breeding plan. This might sound ridiculous, but in reality, it is very important. A breeding plan is something that you should have before you even get the dogs that you are planning on breeding.

A breeding plan should be comprised of several different things. First of all, you need to have an idea of the type of dog that you are going to be breeding. This includes the information that you have already learned about the breed that you have chosen.

Next, you want to look at the breeding standards for that type of dog, and figure out which of the standards you are going to be breeding for with the dogs that you are breeding. A good breeder strives to maintain the breeding standards and will try to breed those elements into his or her dogs.

Next, you will want to have a breeding plan that explores the various ways that the breeding program is going to be set up. Include information about making sure that you have a good questionnaire and a waiting list program, and information about how you plan on screening applications for your puppies to choose good homes.

Your breeding plan should then go into detail about how many dogs you plan on having and where you plan on keeping them. If the idea of putting dogs in your backyard, or having a shed to hold your dogs even crosses your mind, get out of breeding right away. Your dogs should be in your home and should be a part of your family. This is how you produce good puppies.

Your breeding plan should include the ways in which you are going to manage the dogs that you have in your program. It should have information about how many dogs you'll have in your home, and how those dogs will be trained and maintained.

Then, include information in your breeding plan about roughly how many litters you plan on having with the dogs. Keep in mind that you should not breed a female dog each time she goes into season, which means that you will only have one litter a year, at most, for each female dog that you have in your program. A good breeding outfit will pay attention to this and will not breed females in back to back heat cycles.

Your breeding plan also has to have information about how you intend on keeping your dogs up to date on their shots, and the specific training you want to do with them. Don't forget to add information about how you plan on socializing your dogs to make sure that they are prime examples of the way that your dogs should be.

You will want to be sure that you provide enough information in your breeding plan so that you can look back on the plan at a later date and answer any questions that you might have about the way that your breeding program should be working.

There are some things that you should include in your breeding plan so that you know you are going to be successful at breeding.

1. The breed of dogs you are going to own
2. The number of dogs you think you would be able to handle
3. Where your dogs will stay, and what type of accommodations you will offer them
4. The vet you will use
5. The amount of money you have to spend on dog care, vet care, and all of the expenses, and where that money will come from.
6. How many years you plan on breeding dogs
7. Whether you plan on continuing your breeding program with dogs that you breed yourself, or whether you plan on bringing in new dogs to continue your program
8. What you will do with dogs when they can no longer breed for you.

9. How you will deal with complications in pregnancy and with puppies that don't make it.
10. How you will know when you can breed your dogs again
11. How you will know when it is time to stop.
12. Your overall goal for breeding – the types of things that you are looking for in the breed and the types of things that you hope to achieve by breeding the dogs that you have chosen.

If you are able to have a breeding plan that includes these things, you'll find that you have much more information at your disposal than you thought, and you'll be able to make a good decision about breeding dogs in general.

Remember, you want to have a breeding plan that you can change as you see fit, and one that is going to allow you to make a good decision about the types of dogs that you are going to be breeding. It is important to have the right type of breeding plan for your needs, and it is very important to make sure that you can follow through with your breeding plan.

Also, your plan should not be set in stone. There might be things that you want to change about your breeding plan as time goes on, and you should be able to easily change these things. It is going to be important for you to be flexible as a dog breeder, so that you can make good decisions about what is right for you and for your dog.

CHAPTER 4- STUDY BREEDING STANDARDS

In order to do a breeding plan in the correct manner, something that you are going to have to do is to develop an idea about the breed standards that you are looking at and how to apply them to your own dogs.

Looking at breeding standards is a very important way for you to make sure that you are having a responsible breeding program. All of the breeds that exist that are either UKC registered or AKC registered are going to have breed standards that have been developed.

The standards have been developed for each breed by the people who register them and who have bred them for many years. Therefore, these are the standards that are going to be important to you when it comes to making sure that you have been doing the right things in your program.

If you cannot find UKC or AKC breeding standards for your dogs, you might need to look in other areas for the breeding standards. There should be information from the UKC and AKC for those types of dogs. If you are going to be breeding a type of dog that does not have either UKC or AKC standards, you should look for the associations for that breed that you can find in your home country. The associations will help you find the breeding standards.

Once you have the breeding standards, you need to study them carefully. It is going to be important for you to make sure that you know exactly what types of things that you should be looking for when it comes to the dogs that you will be breeding.

The breed standards will talk about physical attributes that you are going to be looking for, and that are important to the breed. This might include a certain color pattern, and a certain idea about the specific markings that the dogs should have. It also should include the ways in which you are going to be looking at things like ear shape, eye shape, and even colors of eyes and coat length.

The breed standards will also contain ideas about gait – which is to say, how dogs that conform correctly to that breed walk and move their body. This is important for you to watch for you in your own dogs.

Breed standards will have both things that you should be looking for when you are breeding the dogs that you want to keep in the breed, and things that you are looking for when you are breeding that you want to keep out of the breed. You should be looking for all of these things when you focus on the breeding standards, because this will help you make sure that you are breeding correctly.

Get a copy of the breed standards and study it, well before you even bring home your breeding stock. This will help you make sure that you know what you are looking for.

CHAPTER 5- OBTAIN YOUR BREEDING STOCK

Your beginning stock is going to be important for you to obtain after you have decided what you would like to breed, and after you have researched the breeding standards that you are going to be looking for.

Armed with a copy of the breeding standards, go to work searching for breeding stock for your own breeding operation. Remember, however, that sometimes you need to alter what you are looking for.

The best way to obtain breeding stock is to do so with puppies. Of course, this means that you are going to need to wait for a long time to start breeding yourself, but you will have the best breeding stock that is possible. Look for breeders that have a good reputation amongst your own breed of dogs, and make sure that these are the types of breeders you are going to be working with.

Then, seek out a male and a female to start with. It is never a good idea to start a breeding program by getting more than two puppies. You are going to want to start small, no matter what you want to do in the future. Find a male and a female from two separate breeders, or from the same breeder if you can be certain that they are not related.

Look at the pedigrees of the puppies before you buy them. You are going to want to be sure that there are no common relatives within a certain amount of generations. For some dog breeds that are small and new you might find common relatives as far back as three or four generations, and that might be fine for that breed. However, for breeds that have been around for a long time, you are going to want to be sure that there are no common relatives for many, many generations.

Again, a look at the breed standards will help you figure out what types of pedigrees you should be looking for in your puppies. You should know that ancestors that have championships are going to produce good puppies, for the most part, and you will be able to be confident in knowing that you have gotten a beginning stock that has championship blood lines.

You should be looking at the pedigrees of the puppies before you purchase them. Then, be sure to follow all of that particular breeders regulations about the dogs and make sure that you have been approved to own them. Pay for the puppies, and bring them home.

You now have the beginnings of your breeding stock. Remember, however, that you have just started on a journey that is going to be a very long journey indeed. It is going to be important that you follow through with your breeding plan and the breeding standards that you have researched so that you can be sure you are providing your puppies with the best home possible.

There are some things that you want to look for in your breeding stock.

1. Temperament.
2. The quality of the dog.
3. The lineage of the dog.
4. Whether or not the dog has been shown. (if you aren't buying a puppy)
5. If shown, what type of championships the dog has received
6. The mother and father of the dog – their temperament
7. If the mother and father were shown, if you are buying a puppy, and if so, what type of championships they have received
8. Where the puppies are raised for the first 8 weeks of their life

9. What the breeder's standards are all about, and what the goal of their organization is all about.
10. What type of training the mother and father have had.
11. What type of situation the puppy was born in.
12. What the puppy looks like – their markings and their colors
13. If the puppies ears are straight and their eyes are bright.
14. If the puppy is friendly.
15. If the puppy will allow you to turn him on his back and scratch his belly while you hold him in your arms – this shows a trust for people and a love for affection.
16. What size the puppy is in comparison to his litter mates – you should choose one that is not the biggest nor the smallest.
17. How the puppy acts with his littermates – you should choose a puppy that is good with the other dogs and that loves being with the other dogs. Don't pick one that doesn't play with the other puppies.

If you choose your breeding stock based on these things, you should be able to have good breeding stock that you can depend on.

CHAPTER 6- BREEDING DOGS CARE

Now you have your beginning stock, and you are going to be able to start on the breeding journey. But first, you get to do the fun part, which is to raise puppies from the start.

The best breeding stock is going to be dogs that have been hand raised by you from puppy hood. This will allow you to socialize the dogs properly, and to be sure that they are kept in such a way that you would be proud to have them produce puppies.

Do all of the regular things that you would be doing for puppies while you are raising your breeding stock. Be sure that they are well socialized, both with each other and with other animals, and people as well. Take your puppies out into the world and make sure that they meet other dogs, other animals and lots of people.

You might also want to do training with your puppies during this time. The more that you work with your breeding stock while they are young, the more likely they are going to be to produce good quality and healthy dogs for you in the future. Make sure that they are potty trained and that they know all of the basic commands.

The most important thing that you want to do with your breeding stock is to make sure that they are well socialized and that they are hand raised. These are both very important things because they will help you see that you need to have dogs that are well bred and very well socialized. This is going to be your number one goal when it comes to raising dogs.

Dogs that are hand raised are going to be better about the puppies that they produce. They will produce good quality puppies and they will allow you to help in the birthing process as you should. Therefore, you are going to want to be sure that you are hand raising your puppies all the way to adult hood.

With some purebred dogs, temperament is the biggest issue that breeders watch out for and that breed standards talk about. Therefore, something that you are going to want to do for sure is to make sure that you have created a situation in which the dogs are very well socialized. This is especially important if you are breeding a dog that is known to be temperamental. You are going to want to make a difference with your dogs.

Also, keep in mind your breeding standards and your breeding plan. What is important to you about the breed of dogs and what do you want to accomplish? You should have already decided on a major goal for your operation. Perhaps it might be to produce puppies that have a line that is known for being well socialized, or perhaps it might be to produce a line that is known for being a good quality of show dog.

No matter what your main goal is, raise your puppies with that in mind. The more that you can develop whatever it is that you are looking for within them, the more that you will be able to know you have a good quality breeding program.

CHAPTER 7- WHEN TO BREED

When you are raising dogs in order to breed them, you are going to need to decide when you should begin the breeding process. This is very important because you don't want to breed dog when they are too young, and you also don't want to wait too long.

There are some good rules to follow when you are deciding when to breed your dogs. First of all, keep in mind that you should be prepared for your dogs to not breed as you would like them to. Just because you have a male and a female doesn't mean that they will breed correctly, and it doesn't mean that they'll produce the puppies that you want them to.

A good rule to follow is that you should never breed a female dog on her first heat cycle, and not even on her second if you can help it. You should wait until she is at least a year and a half old, or on her second heat cycle, whichever comes first. Most breeders wait until the female is two years old to start breeding.

Male dogs can breed when they are at least a year old, although they might not mature fully before then, so you want to keep an eye on your male and make sure that he is the correct age.

Remember if you have a male and a female dog that are living together, you will need to keep them apart during the heat cycles that you don't want them to breed in. Your dogs will breed if they get the chance, because dogs don't know that they are too young, and they won't understand if they have already been bred on their last heat cycle. Therefore, it is up to you to make sure that breeding only takes place when you want it to take place.

The first thing to think about is the age. Then, it is important to think about how often. Responsible breeders won't breed their dogs on back to back heat cycles. So, if your female dog has had a litter of puppies on one cycle, even if she had no problems and the litter was successful, you don't want to breed her on the next one. Be sure that she is kept away from the male dog until you are ready to breed her again.

CHAPTER 8- SORTING POTENTIAL OWNERS

A responsible breeder will have a questionnaire for potential owners, and will also have a waiting list for them. This helps you to provide yourself with a good idea of what owners will be like and it allows you to approve them even before you have puppies.

If you haven't already done so, while you are waiting for your breeding stock to mature and be ready for breeding, it is a good time to develop a web page that you can use to find homes for your puppies. On the page, you should have information about who you are and what you are going to accomplish through breeding. You should also have a questionnaire.

This should be a series of questions that you will ask a potential owner to fill out. This is important to do, because you will want to place your puppies in a good home, not just the home that will pay the most for them. Therefore, something that you need to do is make questions that potential owners will fill out. Remember if someone doesn't want to take the time to fill out the questionnaire about what kind of home they would provide, they aren't going to take the time to provide your puppy with a good home, either.

There are some great questions that you should ask on your questionnaire, so that you know for sure what type of home your puppy will have. Here are some sample questions to get you started.

What is your personal information?

What type of home do you have for your new puppy?

What do you want to get from your new puppy?

Have you read the breed standards?

What types of things are important for your puppy to have?

Do you want a male or female?

Do you plan on breeding your puppy?

Do you plan on showing your puppy?

Where will your puppy sleep?

What food will your puppy eat?

Who will be responsible for taking care of your puppy?

What type of life will your new puppy have?

Will your puppy have an area in your home that is just for them?

Will your puppy get enough exercise?

Do you have children or do you intend to have them?

Will you teach your children about the responsibilities of having a dog?

Will you make sure that your children treat your puppy correctly?

What will you do with your puppy while you are at work?

Do you have a fenced in yard for your puppy to run in?

What type of exercise will your puppy get?

What type of training are you going to have for your new puppy?

What will happen to your puppy if you are no longer able to take care of him?

Would you allow us to come to your home and see where your puppy will be living?

Do you plan on sticking to the breed standards for raising your puppy?

What dogs have you owned in the past, and have you been happy with the breeds?

Which dogs were you not happy with and why?

Why do you want to own one of our puppies?

What do you expect a puppy to provide you with?

What will you give to your new puppy?

Providing a list of questions to your new owners will let them know what type of home you expect the new puppy to have. This is going to be important because it will help you see what type of people are applying to own your puppy. If they fill out the questions and send it back to you, you know that they are going to be responsible because they have taken the time to fill out the answers to the questions. You can also get a good idea of the type of home that they will provide and then you can approve them.

Once you have the questionnaire, you can begin to allow people to fill it out and place them on waiting lists for your puppies. These should be lists that you will contact every so often. When you have a litter of puppies, you can allow people on the waiting list to have first pick at the puppies.

CHAPTER 9- BREEDING ITSELF

Once you have everything set up, you can begin to actually do the breeding process for your puppies.

Again, make sure that the dogs you are breeding are the correct age. You want to be sure that you have waited for the right amount of time, and that the dogs you are breeding are going to be at the prime condition for breeding.

Take your female and your male dog to the vet and make sure that they are ready to be bred. Have them checked out, and make sure that they are in the right health to breed. Get them up to date on their shots so that you know you will be breeding dogs that are healthy and will not have any shot problems to worry about.

Then, you can let nature work its magic. Your female dog will go into season about two times a year. This will be different depending on the breed. You will know that she is going to into season because there will be discharge that is noticeable from her. Anywhere from 5 to 10 days after you notice the discharge, the male dog will be interested in her. Most of the time, male dogs are interested in the female well before she is interested in them, so don't be discouraged if it doesn't happen as soon as you would like to happen .Simply allow your dogs to be alone together, and when the time is right, they'll take care of the business.

Most breeders don't do any assisting when it comes to the actual breeding. However, with some smaller breeds, or with females that need encouragement, some minor assistance, like holding the female in place, is required. You will need to experiment and see if your dogs need any assistance, or if they are ready to breed right away.

Once your dogs have bred, you will need to treat your female as if she is pregnant. For the first four weeks, keep her on her regular diet, but make sure that she has access to food whenever she is hungry. Don't get her too excited and allow her to do what she would like to do. Keep exercising her, however.

For the second eight weeks, switch your pregnant dog to puppy food .This will help her get the right nutrients. Don't do this before the 5th week, however, as her body needs to produce several things at the start of her pregnancy to be healthy – and as puppy food might not allow this to happen.

Let your mama dog do what she wants to do, and keep in mind that she might be moody or more loving than usual. Keep her with you and keep her exercising as well. This is very important to good development of puppies.

CHAPTER 10- BIRTHING

When it comes time to birth your puppies, there are a few things that you should know so that your puppies can be happy and healthy and that your mother dog will be safe.

First of all, keep track of the due date. Your vet can help you with this, and so can information regarding your specific breed.

As the due date comes closer, be sure that you are gathering your supplies. Your mother dog should have a birthing box that she can go to. Make sure that this is in the room where you want your puppies to be born. It should be in a room that you go in often, like your bedroom – and if possible, it should be in the place where your mother dog sleeps at night. This will allow her to be comfortable with the puppies.

As it gets closer, put together a birthing kit for yourself.

Clean rags

Gloves, if you want them

Iodine

Scissors

Eye dropper

Infant nose and mouth cleaner

q-tips

a scale

Make sure that the mother is comfortable in her birthing box and then, wait.

When the time gets close, you'll be able to tell. Your mother dog will spend more time nesting in her box. As she goes into labor, she'll usually sit up and pant. You'll be able to see the contractions that she is having in her body.

Move her to the birthing box and then wait with her. Most mother dogs don't like to have puppies alone if they have good relationships with their owners.

As the puppies begin to be born, you will have to decide whether or not you want to assist. Most of the time, nature can take its course, and the mother will deliver the puppies.

If the mother is laboring for more than an hour after you have seen the sac and the puppy has started to be born, you will want to call a vet to help you. The puppy might be stuck. Otherwise, you can gently guide the puppy out by pulling gently but firmly with a soft and damp rag. Try not to break the sac open while the puppy is still inside of the mother dog. If the sac does break, you'll need to get the puppy out right away.

Once the puppy is out of the mother, she should break open the sac and lick the puppy's face. If she doesn't do this in a matter of moments, you can break open the sac using your fingernails or a scissors.

Present the puppy's face to the mother and get her to lick it clean. You should hear the puppy begin to breathe. If the mother doesn't lick the puppies face, you might need to clean it for her and clear the puppy's nose and throat. You can do this by using the rag or the infant cleaner. Most of the time, the mother will clear the passages so the baby can breathe.

In between puppies, the mother should clean up most of the mess and should clean the baby. Try not to get in her way unless she is having problems with something. You can put the puppy onto a nipple while she does this. Healthy puppies should want to suck right away.

Most puppies will be born within a couple of hours of each other. If the mother dog is laboring and it has been more than a couple of hours between puppies, you should call a vet because there might be something wrong.

Once all of the puppies have been born and the mother is no longer laboring, you can weigh the puppies and change the bedding in the box. The mother will probably want to go outside to go to the bathroom. When she comes back, be sure that you put the puppies onto the nipples to eat.

Your main goal should be to assist the mother if she needs it. Check on them from time to time. It is always a good idea to move puppies closer to the mother if they have been moved, and to put them on a nipple so that they can eat.

There are some things to watch out for right away when it comes to puppies. You should seek vet help immediately if:

A puppy doesn't eat

A puppy isn't moving around

A puppy is being pushed to the side by the mother

A puppy is noisy.

Healthy puppies should:

Stay mostly quiet

Gain weight each day

Be actively eating

Breathe at a normal rate

Seem content.

CHAPTER 11- RAISING PUPPIES

For the next eight weeks, you are going to be in charge of making sure that the puppies are raised correctly. It is going to be your job to make sure that the puppies you are providing are properly socialized and healthy.

First of all, they should be taken to the vet sometime after they are born. However, you want to make sure that they don't get too cold or too hot, so make sure that this isn't right away. For the first few days, leave them with their mama and try not to bother them too much.

However, you should handle the puppies. A mother dog that knows you and that trusts you will allow you to pick up the puppies, to weigh them daily, and to pet them. You want the puppies to grow up being used to being held and you want them to recognize you right from the start.

Adults should handle the puppies after they are born .Don't take them out of the mother's sight, and don't keep them any longer than she can stand. If she starts to get nervous, put the puppies back. However, be there with them and her often, so that she can get used to you and so that she can get used to someone else handling the puppies. This is very important if you want to be sure that the puppies grow up well socialized.

Continue to handle the puppies and to weigh them each day. Make sure that they are gaining weight, and if a puppy is not, seek the advice of your vet right away. When they are a few weeks old they should visit the vet just to make sure that they are healthy.

The puppies will be blind and deaf for several days after they are born. They should begin to hear you within a few days, and should open their eyes in about a week. Puppies will grow very quickly, and will look different from one day to the next.

The best thing that you can do for the puppies is to make sure that you are present ,that you are holding them each day, and that the mother has good food, clean water, and plenty of exercise and love. This is the best way to make sure that the family is healthy.

As the puppies get older, they will open their eyes and begin to be able to walk around. This is a good time to star to introduce them to other people.

Because you are going to be finding homes for the puppies, make sure that you are socializing them to everything. In order to socialize a puppy to something have them experience it.

Keep them in a room with a TV or radio on.

Have a ringing phone nearby.

Have children hold them

Have adults hold them.

Allow them to walk and run on different surfaces

Speak in loud voices and quiet ones

Have animals (who can be trusted with puppies) meet them – cats, guinea pigs, etc.

Make sure they interact with the mamma dog and with other dogs that you might have.

There are some things, however, that you should not let your new puppies do.

Don't expose them to dogs other than your own until they have had their puppy shots.

Don't take them to the dog park until they have had puppy shots.

Don't let people handle them unless they have washed their hands.

Don't let the puppies get too cold or too hot.

Keep them out of drafts and away from windows.

Don't get them overly excited

Don't keep them away from their mother for more than a few minutes as long as they are nursing.

Don't let them eat anything other than puppy food as they get old enough.

Raising puppies for the first 8 weeks can be interesting and time consuming .There are a few things that you will need to be sure that you start to do for the puppies so that you can be sure you are providing the people who buy your puppies with a good dog.

Get them socialized to a collar and leash

Take them for short walks

Start to work on potty training

Get them eating canned and solid puppy food, after their teeth come in, around 6 weeks.

Socialize, socialize, and socialize!

Then, your puppies should be ready for their new homes!

CHAPTER 12- WAITING LISTS & INTERVIEWS

Once you know how many puppies you have, and whether they are male or female, you will have some decisions to make as far as what you want to do with the puppies. Sometimes, you might want to keep one for yourself. Many breeders will keep a female that they think is good for their program, and then bring in a new male later on to continue their program. You also might want to keep one for reasons other than breeding.

When you know what dogs you aren't keeping, you can start to go through your waiting list to see what types of homes are going to be available for your puppies. It is important for you to know how you will be providing puppies to your waiting list – is it a first come, first serve situation, or do you have other ways of matching puppies with homes?

After you know which people on your waiting list will be able to have the puppies, you'll need to contact them and tell them what you have, and see if they are interested. This is a good time to have them come to your home so you can meet them and they can pick out the puppy that they would like to have.

Remember, just because someone is on your waiting list does not mean that they'll want a puppy, and it also does not mean that you owe them a puppy. If someone comes by and you don't like them – if you don't trust them or don't like the way that they act around the puppy, there is no reason that you can't say you aren't going to give them a puppy. Remember, these are your puppies and your job is to make sure that they go to the best homes possible. Therefore, don't be afraid to be picky.

After you have approved of homes and people have chosen their puppies, you can ask for a deposit to hold that particular puppy.

Then, you can continue to raise the puppy until you feel that they are old enough to go to their new homes.

CHAPTER 13- WHEN TO BRING PUPPIES TO THEIR NEW HOMES

It is important for you to make sure that the puppies are old enough before you let them go to their new homes. You want to wait until they are at least 8 weeks old, but also until they are fully weaned. Some breeds take longer, and some breeders like to have the puppies stay longer so that they can be sure they are healthy.

No matter what you decide for yourself, it is important to continue to train and socialize the dog while they are with you. By 8 or 10 weeks old, a puppy should be having a good idea of what it means to go potty outside, and should be eating on their own. Then, you can feel free to have them go to their new homes. Just make sure that you feel ready and that you think the puppies are ready.

Remember that sometimes the mother dog has things to teach the puppies even after they have been weaned, so you might want to wait for this to happen.

CHAPTER 14- MAKING CONTRACTS

It is always going to be important to have contracts when you are dealing with puppies.

You want to make sure that you have a good owner contract that you can refer to, which will outline what the new owner should be doing with your dog. You might include things such as a puppy back system, where if the new owner breeds the dogs, you have the right to get a puppy back if you would like.

Also, you might want to consider a clause that states that the puppy should be returned to you if the new owner can't keep it. This will help you be responsible. Remember that this isn't just an item that a person is buying from you, it is a life – so you need to make sure that you contract states this and that your contract is done correctly.

There are several things to include in puppy contracts.

Puppy Back?

What happens if an owner can't keep the dog?

Can the dog be shown?

Does the dog need to be neutered/spayed?

How should the dog be treated?

Can the dog be kept outside or does it need to live inside?

How much does the puppy cost?

Is the breeder responsible for anything during the puppy's life time?

What is the new owner responsible for?

Creating a contract can help you make sure that you have enough information and can give you the peace of mind that you need to assure yourself that the puppy is going to be well taken care of.

The contract should be signed by all of the parties that are involved, and you want to be sure that you are notarizing the contract. Remember that no matter how nice the transaction might seem to be, there might be problems that develop, so a contract is always a good idea, no matter what.

Checking Up on Puppies

Something else that you will want to do with your puppies is to always check up on them. Many contracts include statements that the new owners have to provide the breeders with pictures or information for a certain amount of time. This is done for many reasons. It allows you to keep control over the puppies, and it allows you to make sure that you take responsibility and that they have gone to a good home. It also allows you to be in control of making sure that the contract is being followed.

Also, checking up on the puppies and seeing how they are allows you to see what type of dogs are coming out of your breeding program. This is going to give you a good idea of whether or not your own goals are being met, and of whether or not your breeding program is a success.

Chapter 15- Know The Facts

Once you've gone through a litter of puppies and gotten them off to good homes, you might be concerned with when it will be time to breed again. It is very important for you to make sure that you know what you are doing. Do not breed dogs on her next heat cycle after she has had a litter of puppies. You might want to wait a year or more, depending on how hard the pregnancy and litter was on the mother dog. These are all decisions that you should make when you are breeding dogs so that you can be sure you are providing good quality puppies.

Knowing When To Not Breed

Part of being a responsible owner is knowing also when not to breed your dogs. You don't want to breed a dog too soon, but you also might need to make the decision not to breed the dog if she had a difficult pregnancy, had a hard litter, or had problems weaning or taking care of the puppies. A responsible breeder will know when to not breed again.

What To Breed For

There are several things that you want to breed for. When you are looking at the dogs that you hope to breed, and when you are making judgments about those dogs and deciding which ones to breed, you should look for several things.

Temperament – how the dog acts around you, around others, and around other animals or children.

Physical state:

Colors

Size

Ear Shape

Eye Shape, Color

Coat Thickness

Gait

Health

Long life span

Less of a chance of sicknesses

If your dog has these characteristics as called for in the breed standards, you might want to consider breeding them.

What To Breed Out

There are also several things that you will want to breed out. This means that if you have a dog that exhibits these things, you'll want to spay or neuter them and place them in a pet quality home.

Sickness

Weak Joints or Knees

Coats that are not sufficient for breed standards

Improper Gait

Colors or markings that don't conform to breed standards

Wrong shaped ears, eyes, or facial features

Bad temperament

Tendency towards shyness

If your dog has these things, you might want to consider not breeding them, so you don't pass on the traits that you don't want to pass on.

CHAPTER 16- DOG SHOWS

You might decide that you want to show dogs. This is something that many breeders do and that is important to lots of different breeding programs. If you decide that you want to show dogs, there are a few things to keep in mind.

First of all, showing dogs can be a lot of work. You will need to be sure that you have the right forms and information so that you can get signed up for the show early enough. You'll also need to be sure that you are ready to show dogs, meaning that you have had the proper time to work with your dogs.

When you are deciding whether or not to show dogs, there are some questions that you should ask yourself so that you know you are showing the right types of dogs.

Does your dog conform to breed standards?

Is your dog well trained or can you train her easily to walk in the ring?

Is your dog comfortable with someone touching her and lifting her up?

Is your dog comfortable with other dogs?

Will your dog bit or will she try to bother the other animals?

Are you ready to travel to shows with your dog?

Is dog showing something you think you would like as a hobby?

The answers to these questions will help you make sure that you have provided enough information about your dog and that you know your dog is going to be good in the ring. This is something that you are going to want to think carefully about before you show your dog.

Showing a dog can lead to great things for your dog herself. She will be able to be better trained, and as you go through more shows she'll learn even more. Also, you'll be able to control your dog better.

Having championships, or having certifications from being shown is an important thing in the breeding world. Many times people will want to have your puppies if the parents have been shown because it shows that your dogs are great examples of the type of dog that they are looking for.

CHAPTER 17- LIFETIME BREEDING & OWNERSHIP

It is important to remember that owning a dog means you are going to have lifetime breeding and ownership responsibilities. If you are breeding dogs, you are going to need to know that you are responsible for that dog, and you are also responsible for the puppies that come from the dog .This means that as a responsible breeder, one of the most important thing that you can do is make sure that you provide your puppies with a guarantee.

As a breeder, you should be ready and willing to take back any puppies that the new owners cannot keep. This means that you need to be willing to be responsible for any puppies that you sell, no matter how long you are in business for and no matter how long you breed puppies or how man you breed. This will help you to make sure that you are breeding responsibly.

Also, you need to remember that once you have purchased a dog, even with the intent of breeding him or her, you are responsible for that dog. If the dog doesn't match breed standards and cannot breed, or if the dog cannot breed for some other reason, you are still responsible for that dog for the dog's entire life. Therefore, you might end up owning dogs that don't breed. Once a dog is finished breeding for his or her life, you are still responsible for owning that dog, and you need to remember this so that you can be a responsible dog owner.

ABOUT THE AUTHOR

Janet Evans loves children and animals. An expert in child care, she aims to education children and parents in many ways. She has produced many books for children and these books also show her love for animals.

As part of her life, dog care has helped shape her life. Learning many lessons from taking care of dogs, their behavior and the unconditional love they share to their masters. She aims to share her knowledge about these loyal creatures to those who aspire to have a new member in their family.

Lightning Source UK Ltd.
Milton Keynes UK
UKHW020043070821
388396UK00006B/79